Page Turners

D1076859

Irene Barrall

Series Editor: Rob Waring
Story Editor: Julian Thomlinson
Series Development Editor: Sue Leather

HEINLE
CENGAGE Learning

Middlesbrough College

Australia • Brazil • Japan • Ko   nited Kingdom • United States

HEINLE
CENGAGE Learning

Page Turners Reading Library
The Long Road to Lucca
Irene Barrall

Publisher: Andrew Robinson

Executive Editor: Sean Bermingham

Senior Development Editor:
Derek Mackrell

Assistant Editor: Sarah Tan

Director of Global Marketing:
Ian Martin

Content Project Manager:
Tan Jin Hock

Print Buyer:
Susan Spencer

Layout Design and Illustrations:
Redbean Design Pte Ltd

Cover Illustration: Eric Foenander

Photo Credits:
92 (top) Paul Merrett/Shutterstock,
(bottom) Peter Wollinga/Shutterstock
93 (top) nhtg/Shutterstock, (bottom)
Norman Pogson/Shutterstock

ISBN-13: 978-1-4240-4876-2

ISBN-10: 1-4240-4876-1

Heinle
20 Channel Center Street
Boston, Massachusetts 02210
USA

Cengage Learning is a leading provider of
customized learning solutions with office
locations around the globe, including
Singapore, the United Kingdom, Australia,
Mexico, Brazil, and Japan. Locate your local
office at:
international.cengage.com/region

Cengage Learning products are represented
in Canada by Nelson Education, Ltd.

Visit Heinle online at **elt.heinle.com**

Visit our corporate website at
www.cengage.com

Printed in the United States of America
1 2 3 4 5 6 7 – 14 13 12 11 10

Contents

Review

Background Reading

London

Paris

Fontainebleau

Dijon

Bourg-en Bresse

Grenoble

Massa Di Marina

Ciao!

Antibes

Lizzy's Route

People in the story

Lizzy Elliot
an English girl working
in London

Viola Elliot
Lizzy's mother

Tom
a banker who wants to
marry Lizzy

Richard
Lizzy's cousin

Justine
Lizzy's cousin

David Speranza
a friend of Aunt Bea who
accompanies Lizzy on
her journey

The story takes place in England, France, and Italy.

Chapter 1

Wedding bells

It was Monday morning and Lizzy Elliot stepped off the bus, her dark hair shining in the sunlight. She bought a newspaper and a coffee and hurried toward her office in the center of London. At eight-fifteen she stepped inside a modern metal and glass building and took the elevator to the tenth floor. Every detail was exactly the same as every other work day. There was nothing to warn Lizzy that her life would soon change forever.

"Good weekend?" her friend Jane asked as Lizzy took off her jacket and sat down at her desk.

"I watched Tom play football again. In the rain." She smiled and switched on her computer.

"That was it?" Jane asked, shaking her head. "Lizzy, what's the point of living in London if you spend your weekends watching Tom play football and then stay in watching TV?"

Lizzy held up her hand and pointed to the shiny diamond ring on her finger. She had only been wearing it for three weeks, and it still felt heavy and a little strange on her hand.

"We're saving our money, remember? Tom says we should buy a house soon, and then we have the wedding to pay for."

"Have you set a date yet?" Jane asked. Lizzy shook her head. It had been a month since Tom asked her to marry him. He didn't seem in any hurry to plan the wedding, and that was just fine by Lizzy. She wanted time to get used to the idea. It all seemed so adult somehow.

"Well, I think you should enjoy yourself while you can. You have plenty of time to save up for the wedding. Why don't you go on holiday together somewhere exciting?"

Lizzy looked at the rain falling outside the window. A holiday? Now that was a good idea.

She met Tom in their usual restaurant. He gave her a quick kiss before glancing back at the menu. While they waited for their food, he told her about Giles, a friend from work at the bank, who was leaving to go traveling.

"It's a crazy idea," Tom said. "Why does he want to leave such a good job?"

"Still, it must be exciting to go off on an adventure," Lizzy said. "In fact, I was thinking that you and I could go on holiday somewhere."

Tom looked up in surprise. "But we're saving our money for the wedding," he said.

"I know, but there's no hurry. We could go somewhere warm and sunny."

Tom shook his head. "You know I hate the heat. And beaches are my idea of hell," he added.

"OK, so what about a skiing holiday?"

He turned his attention back to the menu. "No, thank you. Dangerous and cold. What's the fun in that?"

"Well, where would you like to go?" Lizzy asked.

"I'm going on a trip to Scotland with the football club in September. I'm not sure if girlfriends are invited, but I can check if you like," he offered.

"No, thanks."

"Don't look so unhappy, Lizzy. I've got a surprise for you. I wasn't going to tell you till later but you look like you need something to cheer you up."

"What is it?" Lizzy asked, leaning forward.

Tom paused and then whispered, "I've found us a house to look at. The appointment's all arranged for tomorrow afternoon at one-thirty. I'll meet you outside your office." He looked at Lizzy's face. "You don't look very excited."

The waiter arrived with their food. Lizzy waited for him to go and then put her hand on Tom's.

"It's a surprise, that's all. I didn't think we'd be looking at houses for a while."

"Why wait?" Tom asked. "And we should start planning the wedding, too. What about September or October after my football trip? We can talk about it tomorrow after we look at the house."

"Yes, let's talk about it tomorrow," Lizzy said and started to eat.

Back in her office, Lizzy told her friend about the house and the wedding plans.

"You don't look very happy about it," Jane said.

"It's all happening a little fast." Lizzy bit her lip and stared at the computer screen. She noticed Jane looking at her. "Don't get me wrong. I want to marry Tom, of course, I mean, who wouldn't? Everyone thinks he's lovely."

"You mean your mother thinks he's lovely," Jane said, crossing her arms.

It was true—her mother, Viola, thought Tom was wonderful. What her mother wanted most for her daughter was a good career and a good marriage. She had always taught Lizzy that it was important to be sensible. And marrying Tom was certainly a sensible thing to do. So why didn't Lizzy feel happier about it?

The phone rang. "That's probably your mother calling to discuss what to wear for the wedding," Jane grinned.

"Shhh," Lizzy said. She listened to the voice at the other end of the phone. After a moment, she whispered, "I'll come right away."

Jane looked at her friend's white face, and her smile disappeared. "What is it, Lizzy? What's happened?"

"That was my mother. She just got the news that my Aunt Bea has died."

"Oh, I'm so sorry. Were you close?"

"Yes. No." Lizzy put her hand on her head. "I haven't seen her for a long time. Sorry, I've got to go, Jane." To her horror she realized that she was about to cry. Before Jane could say anything else, Lizzy picked up her bag and coat and hurried out.

Chapter 2

Aunt Bea's challenge

It had been over twenty years since she last saw Aunt Bea. Her aunt used to stay with Lizzy and her mother on the way back from some exciting place. Lizzy thought she was the most interesting person in the world. She could turn the most ordinary things into an adventure. Though they hadn't seen each other for so long, Lizzy felt a special connection to her aunt.

Lizzy remembered that final visit. It was her birthday, and Aunt Bea arrived with tickets to go and see a show. Later, they returned to the house, tired and laughing. Lizzy's mother was preparing vegetables for their dinner. Her back was straight and tense. Lizzy, looking from her mother to her aunt, knew that something was wrong. Aunt Bea put her finger to her lips, and the laughter stopped.

That night she lay in bed listening to her mother's and her aunt's angry voices downstairs. Walking quietly to the top of the stairs, she sat and listened.

"You have to let the girl have some fun," she heard her aunt say. "Every detail of her life's planned out for her already: school, university, and then some boring office job until she retires. I hope she finds the strength to do something different, otherwise one day she'll wake up and realize that she's never really lived."

"Fun won't help her to put food on her plate or a roof over her head. She's not your daughter, Bea, she's mine." She had never heard her mother's voice sound so cold. Then there was the sound of a door slamming loudly. When Lizzy got up for school the next morning, Bea had gone.

Her mother refused to answer Lizzy's questions. For a long time, whenever she heard the mail being delivered, Lizzy would rush to the door expecting to find a letter written in her aunt's familiar green ink. But years passed without a word. Though Lizzy never forgot Bea, she stopped waiting to hear from her.

Lizzy parked the car outside her mother's house and walked up the path. The front door opened, and her mother appeared.

"I'm sorry I had to give you such sad news over the phone, darling." Her mother's eyes were red.

"How did it happen?" Lizzy asked.

"Come and talk to Bea's friend. He came all the way from Italy to deliver the news. He can answer all your questions."

She took Lizzy inside, where a man was sitting looking at the garden.

"This is David Speranza," her mother introduced them.

Lizzy realized that she had been expecting someone her aunt's age. But David was much younger. He had dark hair and wore a leather jacket.

"I'm very sorry for your loss," he said, shaking her hand. "Bea was a good friend to my parents and to me. I live in a cottage very near her farm."

He waited until Lizzy sat down and then quietly told her that Bea had been ill for over a year. He spoke about Bea's life on a small farm near Lucca in Italy. How she walked and cycled every day in the hills around the farm almost until the end.

"Why didn't anyone tell us she was ill? I didn't even know that she lived in Italy." Lizzy was surprised by the anger in her voice.

"Shhh, Lizzy. It isn't Mr. Speranza's fault," her mother said.

David looked uncomfortable. "I understand that this is a shock for you. But Bea didn't want anyone to know that she was ill. The day before she died, she gave me your mother's address and asked me to deliver a letter to you in person."

He reached in his pocket, took out a letter, and gave it to Lizzy. "Read it and let me know what you decide. Here's my cell phone number. I'll leave you and your mother to talk now. I really am very sorry."

While her mother walked David to the door, Lizzy ran her fingers over the letter. Her heart hurt as she looked at the familiar green ink that she had not seen for so long. Finally, taking a deep breath, she opened the letter and began to read.

Dearest Lizzy,

You have always been in my heart and I think of you often. Don't be sad. I have had a wonderful life and I am in the place that has made me happiest. Lizzy, I want you to have my farm and land in Italy. You are the only person who will appreciate how special the place is. I hope that it brings you the same happiness that it gave me. There is some money, too. My lawyer will give you the details when the time comes. But first you must accept a challenge. I want you to cycle from France to Italy. Your journey will start in Fontainebleau, near Paris, and end at the farm near Lucca. Do you remember my old blue and white bicycle? Well, that's what you will ride as you travel through Europe. One more thing: you can't bring any money on the journey. Don't worry, I know it can be done because this is the journey that I went on when I found my lovely home twenty years ago. As a little girl you were brave and independent and free. That little girl would have loved this adventure. David will help you get started. You need to leave as soon as possible, and he will travel with you as far as Fontainebleau, and then you are on your own.

Have fun, I know you can do it!

With all my love, always,

Aunt Bea

P.S. If you decide not to accept the challenge, then the farm and money will go to your cousins, Richard and Justine.

Lizzy knew that her cousins were only interested in one thing—money. Richard and Justine would probably sell off their Aunt Bea's farm and land without even visiting it. Aunt Bea would have known that, too.

"Oh, very clever, Aunt Bea. Thanks very much," she sighed.

Before Lizzy could put the letter away, her mother returned to the room.

"Can I read it?" Her mother took the letter without waiting for a reply and read it quickly. "Obviously you're not going to do this."

"I haven't had time to think," Lizzy said, taking the letter back.

"You don't need to think about it," her mother said. "It's a crazy idea. You're far too busy at work. And what about Tom? Anyway, it's just not you, darling."

"What do you mean?" Lizzy asked.

"I mean that this sort of thing is for someone like Bea, not a sensible girl like you."

"Yes, that's me—a sensible girl with a plan," Lizzy said, putting the letter carefully into her bag.

Of course her mother was right, as always. Cycling five hundred miles across Europe on Aunt Bea's ancient bike was a crazy idea. Simply crazy.

Chapter 3

Decision time

She didn't sleep well, dreaming that she was at work, and her smart business suit had turned into a white wedding dress. Aunt Bea appeared in the dream, wheeling her old blue and white bicycle. "Come on, Lizzy," she said. "You know you can do it."

When she got to work, she phoned Tom and told him about Bea's challenge. "It's a crazy idea," he said, sounding just like her mother.

"I suppose they're both right," she said later to Jane.

Jane surprised her by saying, "No, Tom and your mother are wrong. This isn't their decision, it's yours. Don't you see? This is a perfect opportunity for you to finally make a decision that isn't sensible and planned. Sometimes there's a look in your eye that says you've been waiting for a chance like this all your life, Lizzy. You probably have lots of holiday left, or you can ask Mr. Carlton for unpaid leave," Jane said.

"How many coffees have you had this morning? I think you've fried your brain." Lizzy shook her head, turning on her computer.

"Fine." Jane picked up the documents from the desk. "But why did your aunt give you this challenge? There must be a reason."

Lizzy sighed. She had been asking herself the same question.

When Jane left, she picked up the phone to call David to tell him that she wouldn't accept Bea's challenge. But something made her put it down again. She would call him after lunch, she promised herself.

At twelve-thirty, she went down to the reception desk on the ground floor of the office block where she worked. Tom had called to ask her to meet him. He said he had a surprise to cheer her up. As she stepped outside of the elevator, she saw her cousins, Richard and Justine, waiting. It was too late to turn back; they had already seen her.

"Lizzy, we heard about poor Aunt Bea. We came to see if you're alright. It was such a shock," Richard said. She looked at him in surprise. Richard was usually never sympathetic. He put his arm around her and started walking toward the door. Justine walked beside him, carrying a small white dog that barked loudly.

"We also heard about your challenge," Richard continued.

"And we can't imagine little cousin Lizzy cycling all the way from France to Italy, can we, Popsy?" Justine said in a baby voice to the dog as she fed it a biscuit.

"Thanks for coming to see me. But I'm late. I'm meeting Tom," Lizzy said, pretending to check her watch.

"This won't take a minute," Richard said, putting his arm out to stop her. "We heard that there's a letter that says that if you don't complete the cycle ride then Bea's farm and her money will go to Justine and me."

"How do you know about the letter?" she demanded.

He tapped a finger to his nose. "I have my contacts."

Lizzy could guess who the "contact" was. Her mother probably telephoned Richard after she left. The cousins always seemed able to fool Viola into thinking they were wonderful and kind.

"Listen, we'll make this easy for you. Contact Mr. Speranza and tell him that you aren't going to cycle to Italy. Justine and I will get the money and the house, and we'll share the money with you. So, you get around 150,000 euros for doing nothing. You don't even need to go near a bike." Richard looked pleased with himself.

"Of course, Richard and I get the farm and land in Italy," Justine said quickly.

"Yes, of course," Richard agreed.

"What makes you think that I won't cycle to Italy?" Lizzy asked, smoothing her skirt.

The brother and sister looked at each other and laughed.

"Tell me, what makes you so sure that I can't do this?" she repeated.

"Lizzy, cycling from France to Italy is simply not a sensible thing to do. And we all know how sensible you are. Your mother phoned me this morning and asked me to make sure that you didn't do anything silly. I advised her to call Mr. Speranza right away to say that you had decided not to accept Bea's challenge. He should be traveling back to Italy right now."

"Careful, you almost stepped on my poor little Popsy," Justine said crossly as Lizzy stood and stepped over the dog.

"Hey, where are you going?" Richard called.

Lizzy didn't reply. She was already walking quickly back toward the office.

Tom was waiting outside the building when she arrived. He was looking at his watch.

"Lizzy, you're late. I've arranged for us to look at the house I told you about. We have to get a taxi right now." He started to walk away but stopped when he realized that she wasn't following him. "Come on, what are you waiting for?"

"Well, I'm going to accept Bea's challenge." Lizzy didn't realize that she intended to say the words until they were out of her mouth.

"But that's mad!"

"Tom, I've never really done anything that isn't planned or sensible, and this might be my last chance."

"But I don't understand. What's wrong with being sensible? It's one of the things I like most about you."

"Like?"

"Love. I mean it's one of the things I love most about you. And what about our plans? What about the wedding?" He ran his hand through his hair.

"Tom, I'm cycling to Italy, not going to the moon. I'll be back in a few weeks."

"The Lizzy that I want to marry wouldn't leave in the first place." Tom's voice was cold. "I just don't know you at the moment. Look, I suggest you think very carefully about this." Without waiting for a reply, he turned and walked away.

Lizzy's boss was also unhappy with her request to take unpaid leave.

"I always thought you were a sensible, reliable sort of girl. Someone I expect to go far in this company."

"I haven't taken a vacation since I started with this company, Mr. Carlton. This is a once in a lifetime request, and Jane has agreed to look after my projects."

He leaned back in his chair and tapped a pencil on his desk. For a moment, Lizzy thought he might fire her.

"You can have six weeks and not a day more. Do you understand? Without salary," he added quickly.

Her next task was to phone David. When she told him that she had decided to accept the challenge, he sounded surprised.

"Your mother telephoned. She said you didn't want to do it."

"It wasn't her decision to make."

"OK. Meet me at St. Pancras station tomorrow at nine. We'll take the train to Paris."

Lizzy spent the rest of the afternoon making arrangements and tidying her desk. Just before she left, an e-mail arrived from Tom. She read:

If you go on this stupid journey then the wedding is off. Tom.

Taking a deep breath, Lizzy wrote in reply:

If that's what you want. Good-bye, Tom.

She hit "send" before she could change her mind.

As she hurried out of the building, Richard and Justine were waiting for her.

"We need to talk, Lizzy. Where are you going?" Richard demanded as they hurried along beside her. Lizzy held up her hand. A taxi slowed to a stop.

"Sorry, I'd love to stay and chat but I have a train to catch." Lizzy got in and closed the door. As the taxi drove off, she smiled at the surprise on her cousins' faces.

Chapter 4

The great outdoors

The train to Paris was crowded with excited travelers. David and Lizzy found their seats and arranged their bags.

"I was a little surprised that you decided to accept Bea's challenge," David said as they sat down. "When we first met, I was pretty sure you would refuse."

"I don't see why you're surprised. I'm an independent woman, and this is just the sort of adventure that I love," Lizzy informed him with more confidence than she felt.

"Have you followed the instructions and left your cell phone and credit cards at home?" he asked, and she nodded. It felt strange traveling without them.

His phone rang, and he answered it. "It's for you," he said, handing the phone to Lizzy.

"Yes? Oh, hello, Mother. I know, I'm sorry I didn't call you. No, I haven't lost my mind. Could you please stop shouting? Look, I can't speak now. I'm on a train. What? Of course, I'll be careful. Please stop worrying."

When she finished the call, she saw that David was watching her, smiling.

"Stop grinning like that," she said, crossly.

"Your mother didn't sound very sure about your independence and love of adventure," he said.

A moment later, his phone rang again. "That will probably be your mother to check that you remembered to pack warm socks and a toothbrush." His face was serious, but there was laughter in his brown eyes. His smile quickly disappeared as he spoke into the phone in Italian. When he finished the call, he threw the phone on the table.

"That was Bea's lawyer. There's been a change of plan. I was supposed to go with you only as far as Fontainebleau. But someone called him and said that the challenge is unfair because you will cheat; the person said that you will not follow Bea's rules. So now the lawyer says that I must follow you on your trip to check that you complete the journey correctly." He folded his arms and stared out of the window.

"Who said that I'll cheat?" Lizzy demanded.

"I have no idea. But this wasn't the way I planned to spend my summer."

"Do you work for this lawyer?" she asked.

"Of course not. I'm a photographer," he said.

"So, you can just say no."

"No, I can't say no. Out of respect for your aunt, I must make sure that the journey is completed correctly."

"You're hiding something. Why can't you say no to Bea's lawyer?"

This time it was David's face that went red. "Because Bea's lawyer is also my father," he finally admitted.

"So you're doing a little task for Daddy? Very adventurous," Lizzy laughed. Suddenly a thought occurred to her. "Wait, does this mean you're going to follow me all the way to Lucca?"

"Yes, and I'm as unhappy about it as you are," David said. They hardly spoke for the rest of the journey. Lizzy took out a map and studied it. *I must be mad*, she thought. *It's bad enough cycling across Europe, but now I have an unfriendly stranger following my every move.* She glanced at David, who was checking his text messages, and wondered if it was too late to change her mind. Then she imagined the pleasure on her cousins' faces when she returned home after only a day. In her head she could hear her aunt saying, "Come on, you can do this, Lizzy." But Lizzy wasn't so sure.

When they arrived in Paris, they took the metro to the Gare de Lyons, the large train station in the center of Paris. From there, they took the train to the town of Fontainebleau. By the time they arrived in Fontainebleau, it was late afternoon. David took her to his friend Claude's apartment. It was in a narrow street, near the center. He showed her to a small garden where flowers and tomatoes grew in pots. In the corner stood a bicycle. Lizzy walked up to it slowly. It was just the same as she remembered: bright blue with white flowers painted on it. There was a basket at the front and two bags on the back.

"I remember Aunt Bea painting those flowers on it. I named it Daisy for her." She reached out and touched it.

A powerful motorbike was also parked next to it. "Who does that belong to?" she asked.

"That's what I'll be following you on. It's easier on the legs," David grinned. "Now can I have all the money in your purse, please?" He took the money. "I'll give it back to you when you complete the journey or go home, whichever comes first," he said.

"I appreciate your confidence in me. Look, how will I pay for a hotel tonight if I don't have any money?" she asked.

"No need for a hotel," he smiled. He pointed to the bags at the back of the bike. "Daisy is carrying everything you need. There's a tent and sleeping bag in there. Come on, we'll find a field and you can camp."

She hurried to keep up with him. The bike, she now realized, was much heavier than modern bicycles. She could feel her arms ache as she pushed it through the pretty town. Eventually, the road took them away from the town toward the forest.

"That looks like a good spot." David pointed to a place behind some trees. "Do you want me to show you how to put up the tent?"

"No, I can do it myself, thanks." Lizzy pulled the tent from the bag. She was annoyed that he thought she couldn't do anything practical. How difficult could it be? Fifteen minutes later, she was pushing her hair from her eyes, trying to work out what to do. The tent was still not up, and it started to rain again. David put down the book he was reading. "Need any help?"

Lizzy nodded, her face red. Together they put the tent up in ten minutes. He built a fire and made Lizzy some soup.

"Your first meal. Buon appetito!" He wiped his hands and stood up.

"Is there enough for both of us?" Lizzy asked.

"I'm going to a restaurant with Claude, thanks."

"Aren't you camping, too?"

"My job is to make sure that you do the journey as Bea wanted. It doesn't mean that I have to live in a tent, too."

Lizzy watched him leave and then ate the soup, watching the shadows in the forest as they got longer and darker. As soon as she finished, she hurried inside the tent and climbed inside her sleeping bag. Rain hit the outside of the tent. The wind moved through the trees, and somewhere in the forest there was the sound of a branch breaking. She held a fork in her hand in case any mad murderers happened to be passing. She imagined Tom in his nice warm apartment, eating dinner and watching TV. She could be with him now rather than sitting alone in this horrible tent. *So this is what adventure feels like,* she thought, as she lay with her eyes open. Suddenly she felt a long way from home.

Chapter 5

The one that got away

It was the noise that woke her. A strange coughing sort of noise. Lizzy opened her eyes and realized that she was still holding the fork. Pale sunlight was coming in through the tent. She got out of her sleeping bag and looked outside. The sun shone on the leaves of a large oak tree. And under the tree were three wild pigs. They were small and brown. On the back of each one, a line of dark hair stuck in the air. Their shiny black eyes looked up nervously at Lizzy.

"Don't be scared," she said, getting out of the tent. She wished she had her camera with her. Who said she couldn't do adventure? She had slept in a forest at night and woke up to find little pigs coming to say hello.

"Here, little pigs, I won't hurt you." Somewhere in the forest something was moving toward them. The pigs looked up with interest. "Is that your brothers and sisters coming to say hello?" She took a step closer, careful not to make any sudden movements. The sound came again, louder this time. Suddenly from behind a tree appeared the largest pig Lizzy had ever seen. The pig put itself between Lizzy and the piglets. It stared at her. Lizzy took a step backward and tripped over the plate from her evening meal. The crashing upset the pig even more. It lowered its head and began breathing noisily. Lizzy got up and looked around for somewhere to run. The leaves under her feet were still wet from the rain, and she almost fell again.

Suddenly a figure appeared from behind the trees, shouting. David ran toward the animals. The mother pig looked at him crossly and then slowly began to walk away, followed by her babies.

"You didn't need to rush in like that," Lizzy said, embarrassed.

David looked at her pale face, untidy hair, and dirty trousers.

"No, I can see you were doing just fine on your own." He bent and picked up the plate. "If you don't wash up after you eat, then don't be surprised when animals come to finish off your meal."

"That's easy to say when you had a meal cooked for you and a nice warm bed." Lizzy wiped dirt and leaves from her trousers.

"That's true," he said calmly. "Here's some breakfast to help you start your first day." He gave her a bag with some bread, cheese, and fruit. Then he gave her a cell phone. "Here, take this," he said. "It allows you to call me and no one else. Each day when you find somewhere to camp, call me and I'll ride over on the motorbike and check that you are where you say you are."

"So what rules do I have to follow?" Lizzy tore off a piece of bread and ate hungrily.

"Most of the journey has to be on Bea's bike. That means no buses or trains. You can accept a lift, if someone offers, but you can't ask for one."

"What about food? How am I meant to feed myself with no money?"

"Ah yes, I forgot to give you this." He looked inside his bag. "This is Bea's diary from when she did this trip twenty years ago. She said it would give you ideas on where to go and how to survive."

Lizzy took the leather diary. She turned the pages and saw her aunt's neat handwriting. There were drawings too, and some old photographs and maps. It was impossible to speak as she held it in her hands; her throat felt tight, and hot tears filled her eyes. She turned her back and walked away so that David wouldn't see.

By the time she packed away the tent and washed the plate, she was already tired. The bike was heavy with the tent on the back, and she had to cycle with her bag on her back. Cars sped past. "I'm doing my best!" Lizzy shouted as she attempted to get used to the heavy bike. After a while, her balance improved. The first part of the journey was on a gentle forest road, taking Lizzy past sleepy villages with little traffic. But then the road climbed up a hill. Her heart beat quickly as she cycled upwards. At the top, she stopped to take off her rain jacket and took a long drink of water. Sitting at the side of the road, she rested for a while. At last she took out her map to see how far she had cycled. Just six kilometers. *This is going to be a long day,* Lizzy thought.

Late in the afternoon, she found a spot by the river and put up the tent. It was a little easier than the night before. She lay tired and aching on her sleeping bag, listening to the peaceful sound of the water. The silence was interrupted by the sounds of her stomach. There was no food left and after all the exercise, she was hungry. *What would Bea do in this situation?* she wondered. She opened the diary. A page caught her eye:

Money and food all gone now. Caught a fish and cooked it over an open fire. Tasted wonderful.

Lizzy's stomach made a noise. Catching fish. Now that was an idea! She looked around for something to use. Then she remembered that Bea once told her about a man who caught fish with his hands. She walked over to the water's edge and looked down. There was movement under the water, and she saw something silver. Rolling up her trouser legs, she got carefully into the river. The water wasn't deep. Watching carefully, she waited for one of the silver fish to appear and then tried to catch it. But it was too quick and swam away. She walked out a little further; the rocks were smooth under her feet, and it would be easy to slip under the water. She bent down and got ready to try again.

"What are you doing?"

Lizzy jumped at the voice and fell. She turned angrily to see David standing looking down at her.

"Thanks very much. You made me fall in," Lizzy said, pointing to her wet trousers.

"What are you doing?" he repeated.

"I'm getting my dinner." Lizzy turned her back on him and watched the water carefully.

"Look, you have to be skilled to catch fish by hand. You won't get anywhere making a noise like that. It scares the fish."

"You couldn't do any better," Lizzy said.

"We'll see about that." He lowered himself into the water. Confidently, he began walking further along the river. Almost immediately he jumped forward, his arms hitting under the water. When he stood up, he was holding a large silver fish.

"Ha! It took me less than a minute," he called, glancing over his shoulder. But the fish didn't want to be caught; it slipped out of his fingers and fell back into the water. He stepped forward to try to catch it again and tripped over a stone. With a cry of surprise, he went under the water.

Lizzy laughed, waiting until he appeared again so that she could make fun of his fishing skills. But he didn't appear.

"David? Are you all right?" Lizzy struggled to move quickly through the water, which was higher now. She could feel the pull of the current on her legs. "David," she called again, panic in her voice.

A wet hand landed on her shoulder, and she screamed. She turned to face David, who was laughing and wiping water from his face.

"That was a really, really stupid thing to do. I thought you were hurt." She tried to walk away from him, but the fast-running water made it difficult to move anywhere.

"Come on, I've got some food we can share." His long legs made it easy for him to catch up with her.

"No, thank you. I'll catch my own dinner," she said.

"Not everything has to be a competition, Lizzy," he said, pushing himself out of the river and onto the grass. He returned a moment later with a towel. Lizzy turned away as he took his shirt off and dried himself. When she glanced at him again, she saw that he had set up a picnic on a blanket on the river's edge. She could see red tomatoes, bread, and fruit. He sat down and began eating.

"Carry on, you're doing a great job. Mmm, this bread is good," he said. Lizzy pushed her way further down river. The cold was hurting her legs now, and her fingers were blue. She was about to give up when she saw it: a silver blue fish, swimming past her foot. With a smooth movement, she bent down and caught it in her hands. It struggled and almost slipped, but she held on.

"Look, I have my dinner." She held it above her head.

David was on his feet. "You did it," he grinned, leaning over to help her out of the water.

Before taking his hand, Lizzy looked at the fish. It was desperate to get free. She gently put it back in the water and watched it swim away.

"There you go. But if I catch you again, you'll be my dinner," she said, before holding out her hand to let David pull her onto the grass.

"Look, your leg is bleeding. Sit down." He took the towel and began to clean the cut. His hands were surprisingly gentle against her skin.

"That's where you made me fall over. Ow, that hurt."

"Don't be a baby. I need to get it clean. Now go and get dry—you're cold."

She went into the tent and changed her clothes. She could still feel his touch against her leg. She put her clothes on a tree to dry and then joined him at the picnic. The fresh bread and sun-warmed tomatoes tasted better than any restaurant meal she could remember.

"Why did you let the fish go?" David asked.

"I don't know. It didn't seem right somehow. It was struggling so hard to get free," she said.

"And anyway, bread and cheese taste better than a river fish," he smiled.

"Much better," she nodded, and helped herself to another piece of bread. "How do you say thank you in Italian?"

"Grazie," he replied.

"Grazie for this food. So, tell me, why is your English so good?"

"My dad's Italian and my mom's English," he said. She waited for him to offer more information, but none came. David stood and cleaned up the picnic things. "There's enough food in the bag for a couple of days, but then you'll need to find a way to get more." He stood up and wished her goodnight before leaving.

Lizzy watched him go, feeling confused. One minute he seemed relaxed and friendly, but then he closed up again.

After David left, Lizzy sat in the tent and read Aunt Bea's diary.

OK, what have I learned today? Bea wrote. *Well, I'm finding the greatest enjoyment in simple things: the taste of fresh bread, the sun on my back, and a piece of green grass where I can put my tent.*

Lizzy turned off the light and lay down.

Yes, simple things. Maybe this isn't going to be as difficult as I thought, she thought, as she let the sound of the river carry her to sleep.

Chapter 6

An invitation to lunch

When Lizzy woke up the next morning, her throat felt like it was on fire. By the time she packed the tent away, she was coughing. She felt her head; it was hot. When she got back on Daisy, it felt as though every part of her body hurt. She coughed again. This was David's fault for making her fall into the river.

If Lizzy thought the first day's cycling was bad, nothing prepared her for the next few days. Her cold got worse. At times she was so tired that she got off the bicycle and pushed it along the road. "It's just a cold, you're not going to die," David said when she asked if she could spend the night in a hotel. That was all very well for him to say! He was going to go back to a hot bath and a comfortable bed. A warm bath! Just the thought of it made her want to cry. Every part of her body ached now. She wished she was sitting in her little apartment drinking hot lemon juice while in the kitchen her mother made chicken soup to make her feel better.

"Oh, just go away," she said, cycling off.

"Stop acting like a kid. I came to help you find somewhere to stay," he called after her.

"I don't need your help," she said without turning around.

As the shadows grew longer, she saw a farmhouse on a small hill. It seemed to be the only building around. She knocked on the door, and it was opened by a tall man with gray hair. He was eating his dinner and didn't look happy at the interruption. Lizzy used her schoolgirl French to ask if she could camp on the farmer's land. He pointed to a small field behind the farm.

There was no more food. Lizzie wrapped herself in her sleeping bag to keep out the cold. Hoping for some comfort, she opened Bea's diary.

We only find how much courage we have when we go through difficult times, Bea wrote.

Lizzy shut the diary. *Why am I doing this to myself?* she wondered. For the first time since she left London, she really missed Tom. Tom would never leave her in the middle of nowhere with no food.

She was still feeling miserable when a figure appeared outside the tent. Lizzy looked outside and saw the farmer's wife holding a bowl of soup. The woman gave the bowl to Lizzy with a large piece of bread.

The next morning she cycled into the city of Dijon. She found a safe place to leave the bike and walked around the center of the city. Cafés and colorful houses crowded the market square. It was like some cruel joke that she was in a city famous for its food products and yet she didn't have enough money to buy bread. She walked along the side streets and eventually came to an ancient church. On one of its walls she saw a picture of a bird. She looked closer, wondering why it was there.

"If you touch its heart, it's supposed to bring you good luck. I wouldn't touch such an ugly thing for all the luck in the world." The voice was horribly familiar.

Lizzy turned quickly. Her cousin Richard was leaning against the wall, smiling down at her.

"Why is your nose so red?" he asked.

"I'm ill. Why are you here?" She heard the sound of footsteps against stone. Looking over her shoulder, she saw Justine walking toward them, her little dog barking with every step.

"There, there, darling. We'll go to a café and I'll get you a lovely steak for lunch. Oh, hello, Lizzy. We hoped we'd find you." Justine leaned in to kiss the air near Lizzy's cheek and quickly took a step back. "Oh dear, don't they have baths and showers wherever you're staying?"

"I've been camping. In forests and fields. And last time I looked, there was no bathroom attached to my tent."

"Don't upset your cousin, Justine. Can't you see she's not well? Lizzy, will you join us for lunch at our hotel? You look like you could do with a meal."

Though she disliked the idea of spending time in her cousins' company, the thought of lunch in a restaurant was very tempting. And anyway, wasn't it a good way to find out why they were there?

They took her to a smart hotel near the center. Lizzy glanced at the expensive paintings and leather sofas and wondered how much it cost to stay there. At the back of the hotel, surrounded by a quiet garden, there was a restaurant that looked just as expensive. As they took their seats, surrounded by people in smart suits and expensive summer dresses, Lizzy began to feel embarrassed by her cycling clothes.

Richard ordered a bottle of good wine. "Let's drink to family and to Lizzy's success," he said, raising his glass.

"So, why are you here?" Lizzy asked, taking a drink from her glass.

"To see you, of course. Your mother was so worried about you, she asked us to check that you were OK. David has been sending her text messages to let her know where you are, so you weren't difficult to find."

She looked up. Why hadn't David said anything about texting her mother?

"He says you're finding it very difficult, you poor thing," Justine said

"The thing is, Lizzy, you've made your point." Richard poured more wine into her glass. "I admit we were all wrong. You are far more adventurous than Justine or myself. But look at yourself, sweetie. You can't carry on like this."

"And then there's Jane, of course," Justine said, leaning forward and lowering her voice. "What were you thinking trusting her with your projects?"

"Jane? Jane's my friend." Lizzy was finding it difficult to think. She must switch to water. Wine on an empty stomach wasn't a good idea. She was pleased when her meal arrived.

"Don't you think that Jane wants a promotion, too? This is her chance. Not only are you out of the way, but you gave her your most important projects. I heard that Mr. Carlton is thinking of giving her more responsibility." Justine cut off a piece of steak and fed it to her dog.

"How could you possibly know that?" Lizzy's head was beginning to ache.

"Look, Lizzy. This has all been very amusing, but don't you think it's time to come home now? Imagine your own comfortable bed. Mr. Carlton would be so delighted to have you back early that you could persuade him to promote you without any problem."

"And if you come home now, we'll give you half of Aunt Bea's money instead of a third," Justine said, as though talking to a child.

"And the house and land?" Lizzy asked, finishing her chicken.

"That would come to Justine and myself. Come on, Lizzy, it's a generous offer." Richard's voice was impatient now.

"You want to sell Aunt Bea's farm, don't you?" Lizzy said. "I bet you've already spoken to some development company, and they'll turn it into holiday apartments." She saw her cousins exchange a quick glance, and she knew she was right.

"I'm sure we can reach an agreement," Richard smiled.

"No, we can't. I'm going to finish this journey," Lizzy said.

"But look at you. You're a mess. You'll never get all the way to Italy. And when you fail, we get everything anyway. If you turn down our offer now, you won't get a thing," Justine said.

"You'll regret wasting our time." Richard got up and walked out of the restaurant.

"Richard, wait for me." Justine and her dog hurried after him.

Lizzy shook her head as she watched her cousins go. A waiter came over and began to clear the table. "The man who left said to give you this with thanks," he said in French.

It was the bill.

Lizzy tried to explain that her cousins were staying at the hotel, and they were paying for the lunch. The waiter called for the manager.

"I am sorry. There is nobody with your cousins' name staying at this hotel. Now how would Madame like to pay?" the manager asked.

Lizzy looked at the figure on the check. She had spent similar large amounts in the past taking clients to restaurants. But there was no company credit card to help her this time.

"But I don't have any money," Lizzy said.

"That's not a problem. We accept credit cards." He was still smiling.

"But I don't have any cards with me. Nothing. No money and no credit cards."

The manager's smile disapeared. He looked at her untidy clothes and messy hair.

"Then you will please wait here while I telephone the police," he said.

Lizzy watched as he turned to speak into the phone again. The customers at the next table glanced at her and then quickly glanced away. She wondered if it was possible to die of embarrassment. Looking in her bag for her phone, she hoped David would be able to talk her out of this mess. But the phone wasn't there. Justine or Richard must have taken it while she was eating.

The manager stepped away from the table, speaking quietly into the phone. At the same time, the waiter turned to help a customer who had knocked over a glass of water. Without planning it or thinking about it, Lizzy's fingers closed around the handle of her bag. Slowly she got up.

Then she ran.

Ignoring the shouts behind her, she slid across the shiny floor and out onto the street.

Chapter 7

Goats and cheese

Without stopping, she ran to find Daisy. Her hand shook as she took off the bicycle lock. Cycling faster than she thought possible through the streets, at every turn she expected a police car to come after her.

How could her cousins do such a thing? Anger and fear kept her going. The traffic was terrifying, cars coming from every direction. She could feel her heart racing with every turn of the wheel. She had never done anything so criminal in all her life. What would her mother think? Lizzy began to laugh.

At last the buildings and industrial areas were left behind, and she was cycling along open fields. Lizzy could have cried with relief as she realized that she was leaving the city behind. The roads became smaller and quieter. She started to cycle a little slower. For the first time she realized how tired she was. Turning a corner, she came to a beautiful old orchard. In the distance there was the sound of farm animals. A gentle wind made the leaves dance on the apple trees, and the grass under them looked soft and inviting.

She pulled Daisy into the orchard and leaned the bike against an old tree. After the horrible day she had had, this would be a peaceful place to camp for the night. She was unpacking her bag when she found the phone. That was one thing she couldn't blame on her cousins. Happy to have it back, she made a quick call to David and explained where she was. She was careful not to mention her cousins. After what they said about him texting her mother, she didn't

know who to trust. She finished the call and lay down under a tree, lazily taking a bite out of an apple. This place would calm her down, she thought. Throwing the half-eaten apple down on the ground, she put her bag under her head and closed her eyes.

She was just falling asleep when she heard the steps coming toward her. David arrived quickly, she thought sleepily. The steps sounded closer now. She opened her eyes, suddenly awake. A figure was standing over her. Lizzy looked up to see a short, very angry old woman carrying a stick and shouting at her in French. The woman pointed to the half eaten apple on the ground and shouted some more.

"Sorry, sorry. I was hungry," Lizzy said in her best schoolgirl French.

The woman held her arm and made her stand up. Although Lizzy was taller, the other woman was strong and determined. She pulled Lizzy toward a low stone building, shouting all the way.

When David arrived on his motorbike an hour later, he found a very unhappy Lizzy. Her face was dirty, and her hair was a mess.

"What's that smell?" he asked.

"Goat. A mad old lady made me milk them. She uses the milk to make goat cheese. It was horrible."

"Why did she make you milk her goats?"

"Because she says I stole some of her apples. One goat kept trying to eat my hair. And the smell—I'll never eat goat's cheese again." Lizzy made a face. She saw that David was trying not to laugh.

"I really don't see what's so funny!" she said crossly. Then she saw her reflection in the window of the house and started to laugh, too.

At that moment, the old lady came out of the house. David began speaking to the woman in French. The woman obviously liked him, because a moment later she went back into the house and returned with homemade apple juice and small cakes. She pointed to Lizzy and said something to David that made him laugh.

"What did she say?" Lizzy asked.

"She says that you are terrible at milking goats. And she wants to know why my wife needed to steal apples."

"Your wife!" Lizzy shook her head. "Tell her I'd rather marry one of her goats."

The woman introduced herself and asked David another question.

"She says her name is Marie-Helene and she's inviting us to dinner," David said. "Unless you prefer to eat more apples."

Lizzy asked Marie-Helene if she could have a bath. When she came outside again, drying her hair, the table was ready for dinner. It was under the apple trees and had a red-checked tablecloth. The evening was warm, and David was helping to bring food to the table. First they ate chicken and vegetables. After they finished, Marie-Helene brought out her best goat's cheese. Lizzy didn't want to try it.

"It is important to try new things. Even when you are my age," Marie-Helene said. Lizzy tried a little, and it was delicious. They finished with fruit from the orchard. Lizzy couldn't remember enjoying a meal so much.

Marie-Helene said that Lizzy could camp in the orchard. David asked if he could camp, too.

"Aren't you going to find a comfortable hotel in Dijon?" Lizzy asked.

"No, I like the idea of sleeping under the stars tonight. If that's OK with you," he added quickly.

After Marie-Helene went to bed, they sat talking under the trees. Lizzy told David about her cousins and the restaurant.

"Why didn't you call me earlier?" he asked. She was surprised to hear concern in his voice.

"I thought they had stolen my phone. Anyway, I wanted to cycle as far away as I could before the police arrived."

"So, I'm sitting with a wanted criminal?" His eyes shone with laughter.

"I prefer to think that Bea's diary taught me to find creative ways to get out of difficult situations," she said.

For a while they sat listening to the night sounds in the orchard. "Why do you think Bea wanted me to do this?" Lizzy asked.

David thought about the question. "She said that losing contact with you was the saddest thing that ever happened to her. She showed me photographs of you when you were a kid. She said you were always a serious little girl, but that you were brave and adventurous."

"Adventurous, me?" Lizzy couldn't help laughing. "I have a shelf full of travel books that I read in my armchair. How adventurous is that?"

"You didn't have to accept Bea's challenge. But you did. That sounds like the girl Bea knew."

Lizzy was about to reply that she only agreed to the challenge because Richard, Justine, and her mother were so sure that she couldn't do it. But then she realized that this wasn't really true. From the moment she heard what Bea wanted her to do, she had felt excited. It wasn't a serious, sensible, planned decision, and it felt great.

"When I went to visit her as a kid, she always said that we had to try one new thing every day. It drove my mother crazy. She thought Bea encouraged my foolish ideas," she said.

They were quiet for a moment, watching the moon as it disappeared behind a cloud. "How can you be so close to someone and then they just disappear from your life? I didn't even know Bea lived in Italy. Why didn't she ever try to contact me?" Lizzy asked quietly.

"She did." David looked at her, surprised. "She said she wrote you lots of letters, but you never wrote back."

Lizzy sat up. "But I never got any letters."

"Look, maybe you should discuss this with your mother when you get back." He looked uncomfortable.

"My cousin said that you send text messages to my mother to tell her where I am. Is that true?"

"She asked me to. I just tell that you're OK and give her some idea where you are. Sorry, is there a problem?"

Lizzy didn't answer. She knew that it shouldn't be a problem, but what was the point of going on a journey if everyone knew exactly where you are? She still felt like a child with people looking over her shoulder.

"I know you and your mother have some sort of communication problem. So I was only trying to help," he said.

"Communication problem? My mother and I don't have a communication problem."

"You were on the train out of the country before you told her you were accepting Bea's challenge. That doesn't sound like great communication to me," he said.

"It's late. I think I'll go to sleep," she said, standing up and brushing the grass from her clothes. Without looking at him, she went inside the tent.

"Lizzy, I didn't mean to annoy you. But you have to learn to talk about what you're feeling." he said.

"You didn't annoy me, David. I'm just tired," Lizzy said, holding Bea's diary. David was right; there were so many things she couldn't talk about with her mother. They never discussed feelings, and she didn't know where to begin. But one question kept her awake. What had happened to all Bea's letters?

The next morning, Marie-Helene cooked breakfast for them.

"I am going to a village near Bourg-en-Bresse to bring my cheese to a shop there. Would you like a lift?" she asked.

"It's a good idea. You've done a lot of cycling over the last few days," David said.

Bea mentioned Bourg-en-Bresse in her diary, so Lizzy thanked her and accepted.

The truck smelled strongly of goat's cheese, and Lizzy sat next to Marie-Helene's large dog. But she was happy to rest her aching legs. The road climbed higher as they went into the Rhone-Alpes, the green hills with huge sugar-white rocks at the top.

Bourg-en-Bresse was busy when they arrived. "There is a festival this evening," Marie-Helene explained, driving into the center. "There will be music and dancing."

She stopped the truck outside a cheese shop. "What are your plans?" she asked.

"I'll find somewhere where I can work in exchange for food," Lizzy said.

Marie-Helene thought for a moment. "I might be able to help. Wait here." She took the boxes of cheese into the shop and then returned to the truck. When she had finished, she drove to a large old building on the edge of the town. She took Lizzy into a large walled garden where a tall man with a beard was picking vegetables. Marie-Helene spoke quickly to him in French and introduced Lizzy.

"May I present Louis Banon. This is a shared garden for the people that live in the town. Louis is in charge of organizing the jobs here. A lot of people are on holiday at the moment, so they need help. In exchange, they can give you food and a bed for the night."

Louis shook Lizzy's pale, smooth hands. "I don't think you have done very much work outside," he said.

Lizzy admitted that it was true. She looked around the garden. Some people were working on building a wall, others were cutting plants, and some were gathering the vegetables and bringing them into the house.

"You'll be fine," Marie-Helene smiled. "It can't be more difficult than milking goats, can it?"

Chapter 8

Saving the garden

After two hours picking potatoes, Lizzy began to think that milking goats was easy. Her back ached, and her hands were covered in dirt. To make things worse, when Louis came to check her work, he picked up one of the potatoes, shaking his head.

"These are much too small," he said, "and please work faster because we need to get the vegetables inside as quickly as possible."

She stretched and realized that the other workers were watching her. She turned away and bent to start work again.

A bell rang, calling everyone in to eat. The workers sat at a long table. When Lizzy appeared, everyone stopped talking. Lizzy felt uncomfortable. She was aware that people were staring at her.

"Don't take it personally. We don't see many visitors here," whispered a young woman with red hair. "And everyone is worried. They say a bad storm is coming, and if we don't get the fruit and vegetables inside, then a lot of the food will go bad. These people have worked so hard, and we could lose everything."

Lizzy discovered that the girl's name was Sandrine and she was Louis' daughter. Sandrine explained that a group of people in the town used the gardens to grow food together. They only took what they needed, and the rest was given to poor families in the area. They also sold some of the food at

local markets, and the money went into educational projects so that city children could learn about growing their own food.

"It's a good idea, but it's hard work," Lizzy said.

"This is the most important time to pick the fruit and vegetables, but we don't have enough people who want to help." The girl smiled. "So it is very nice that you have come. Tomorrow we hope to bring in the last of the food before the storm comes. Everyone will be much happier then."

"I won't be here tomorrow," Lizzy replied. "I have to leave."

"Oh, I see." Sandrine looked disappointed.

When they went back to work, one of the women showed her how to hold the tools, and another showed her how to pick the vegetables quickly. Back in London, gardening was something that Lizzy avoided, thinking she was no good at it. But as the afternoon went on, she became more confident. Louis came over and watched her. "Good. This is much better," he said "We will make a farmer of you."

Later, Sandrine showed Lizzy to a small, clean room with a bed and a chair. Lizzy lay on the bed and read what Bea had to say about the town:

I sat in the town square and sang songs with a hat by my feet to catch money. In a little while, people gave enough for me to buy my dinner. Later, I heard music. There was a wedding party, and a band was playing. They invited me to join them, so I kicked off my shoes and danced under the stars.

Lizzy smiled. She loved the way Bea jumped into any situation and enjoyed it. Before she could read more, there was a knock at the door. Sandrine appeared, wearing a green party dress.

"Would you like to go to the festival in the town?" she asked. "It'll be fun." Lizzy really wanted a hot bath and bed, but she tried to follow Bea's example.

"I'd love to go," she said. After phoning David and arranging a time to meet, she changed into a clean dress and walked into town with her new friend.

The park was crowded now, and Lizzy couldn't find David. After waiting awhile, she took a walk around the town, watching people get ready for the festival. A group of people were having a picnic on the grass, and they invited Lizzy to join them. One young woman said that she had studied in London.

"There's a party this evening. Why don't you join us?" she asked.

Lizzy accepted; it would make a welcome change from picking vegetables. She imagined herself dancing like a character in a novel.

She returned to the meeting place and found David waiting. He apologized for being late and explained there had been a problem with the motorbike. The lights in the trees looked magical, and the grass was crowded with people dancing. Excited by the thought of a party, Lizzy asked David if he would like to go too.

"Maybe, but first let's see if you can dance." Taking her hand, he led her to the center of the dance floor. He was a surprisingly good dancer, she discovered.

"Wait," she said. Reaching down, she took off her shoes and kicked them to one side and danced in her bare feet. "That's better," she smiled.

She felt something wet against her face. Looking up, she noticed dark clouds gathering in the sky. There was the sound of thunder in the distance, and blue lightning lit the evening sky. The storm was coming.

Large drops of rain were already beginning to fall. People laughed and began to run for cover.

"I'll give you a lift back to the farm. You can get ready for the party," David called over the thunder.

When they arrived, Lizzy ran upstairs to wash her face and brush her hair. Before she left, she took a quick look in the mirror and ran downstairs to meet David.

They were about to leave when she saw Sandrine running down the stairs. She had changed out of the summer dress she wore to the festival and had on an old pair of trousers.

"The rain will make all the fruit and vegetables go bad. We have to get them inside," she explained. Lizzy noticed that more people were starting to arrive. She looked out at the garden. The rain was falling heavier now. The helpers bent over the plants and put the food into baskets.

"Go to the party. I'll stay here and help," David offered.

"No, they need all the help they can get here." She took a basket and they walked out to the wet garden.

Working side by side, they began to fill it with vegetables. Lizzy's dress was soon covered in mud.

"That's an interesting look for a party," he grinned, water running down his dark hair.

There were shouts from the end of the garden. They ran over to find a group of men standing with their hands pressed against the wall.

"The river is getting high," Sandrine shouted above the sound of the thunder. "If the wall comes down, the whole garden will be under water."

"I saw sand at the back of the garden," Lizzy suggested. "Are there any sacks to put it in?"

Sandrine spoke quickly to her father. "Come with me. I'll show you where they are."

The two women ran to collect the sacks while the men brought the sand to the wall. They worked together to fill the sacks with the sand. There was another crash of thunder, and lightning lit the sky.

"We have to hurry," David shouted. "We need to put the sacks at the bottom of the wall to make it stronger. Hopefully that will stop the water getting through."

It was almost morning before the last baskets of food were brought in. The tired workers sat around the table in the mud-covered kitchen. Every surface was filled with boxes of fruit and vegetables. The rain had stopped, and outside the garden was bare. Lizzy rested her head on the table.

"The party is probably still going on. Do you want me to take you?" David asked, drinking a cup of strong, hot coffee. But Lizzy didn't answer. She was already asleep.

Chapter 9

Mountain storm

Lizzy stayed an extra two days to help at the farm. There was still a lot of work to do cleaning up the mess after the storm. Despite her aching back, she was surprised at how satisfying it was to help get the garden back in order. When it was time to leave, Sandrine gave her a bag of fruit and food for the journey. Louis and the rest of the garden workers came out to wave good-bye.

Over the following week, travel became more and more difficult. As she approached Grenoble, all the roads seemed to point upward. The sun and wind turned her skin brown. As she cycled into the mountains, her aching legs felt every mile.

She cycled upward along a narrow road. Looking over the side, she saw there was a sharp drop down the mountain. Cars raced past her, and she struggled to cycle any higher. She got off her bicycle and sat on the edge of the road, unable to go any farther. David appeared. "You're doing well, this is tough cycling country," he said, helping her push the bicycle to the top. He gave her some chocolate before leaving to collect his motorbike. Surprised by his sudden kindness, she put a piece into her mouth and felt the sugar give her a little extra energy to get up the next hill.

When she read Bea's diary, her aunt wrote about the beauty of the mountain roads. She probably had fewer cars speeding past her, Lizzy thought, glancing down at her aching legs.

On a good day, the cool air and sudden silence made her feel as though she was on the top of the world. But on a bad day, she thought she never wanted to see another hill again, ever.

One morning, David arrived as she was packing up the tent and getting ready for another day on the road.

"I got a text from your cousin for you. He says he's worried about your mother." David came over and gave her the phone. She read Richard's text:

Unable 2 contact yr mother. Is she OK?

Lizzy immediately felt guilty. With all the excitement of the last few days, she had completely forgotten her mother. She called her number on David's phone, but there was no reply.

Beginning to feel concerned, she asked David if she could use his phone to call her friend Jane at the office. Lizzy explained the problem, and Jane promised to drive past and check on her mother on her way home. She wanted to know all about Lizzy's journey.

"I'm so jealous. We're all here doing exactly the same things as when you left, and you're out there doing something new every day."

"How is everything going at work?" Lizzy asked.

"Mr. Carlton keeps saying that he wishes you were back. It was a good idea to do this, Lizzy. They're finally realizing just how much you do in this department."

"Thanks for everything, Jane." Lizzy realized how much she had missed Jane's voice.

Once again her cousins were playing mind games, she realized. They planted an idea and then let her imagination do the rest.

Jane phoned back a little later to say that there was no answer at her mother's house.

"Perhaps I should fly home to make sure she's all right," Lizzy said to David that night.

"No. Let me make a few calls to see if I can find out what's happened," he said.

David arranged for the police to go around to her mother's house to check. Eventually they found a neighbor who had a spare key. But inside there was no sign of Lizzy's mother.

"This is completely unlike her," Lizzy said. "She only goes away once a year, and that's always to the same hotel at the seaside. I already phoned the hotel, and they haven't seen her."

"Keep calm, carry on with the journey and I'll keep trying. I'll come and find you as soon as I hear anything. Your mother will be all right."

Lizzy bit her lip. She wanted to believe him, but what if he was wrong?

Twenty miles outside Grenoble, she decided to rest for the night. Every part of her body ached, every bone felt tired. She had just finished putting up the tent when lightning lit the sky. She quickly got inside and listened to the storm move around the mountain.

The noise outside the tent was so loud that she jumped when David's head suddenly appeared.

"Come with me. It's too dangerous to sleep out here tonight," he shouted over the wind.

Lizzy ran with him to the motorbike. She hesitated before getting on. "I don't want to leave Bea's bike," she said. It felt like a part of her now.

"I'll hide it behind these rocks. Now get on the motorbike. We have to get out of this rain."

David drove them along a narrow road to a mountain hut used by walkers. It was a simple wooden building. But it was warm, and they were out of the rain. Lizzy unpacked the bag of food that Sandrine had given her. David lit a lamp, and it turned the light in the hut to a soft gold. They found blankets and were soon warm as they ate dinner and listened to the storm outside.

"So, tell me about working for your father," Lizzy said as David cleared up after the meal.

"I don't work for him," David said. Then he saw Lizzy grinning. He laughed. "OK, OK. You got me," he said. "Well, I already told you my mom is English and my dad's Italian."

"And?"

"And they divorced when I was still at school. I guess Dad always expected me to follow him into the family business. So I studied law at university in Bologna. But then I realized that I was bad at law but good at photography. My mom is an artist, so I think my dad thought I was taking her side." Lizzy nodded in sympathy. "Although I don't work for Dad, I do try to help him out when he has too much work. It makes me feel better."

"Even when it includes following a strange English woman on a bike journey through Europe?" Lizzy asked.

"Let's just say it'll be a long time before I help my father again," he smiled. This was the most relaxed that Lizzy had seen him.

"I can see why you didn't like the idea. Is there someone waiting for you in Italy?" Lizzy felt her face go red as she asked the question.

"A girl, you mean. No, it's not that. I have a photography show in Florence next month, and there are a lot of things to do to prepare for it. I wanted to do everything to see that Bea's last wishes were carried out, because she was the person who persuaded Dad to accept my career change. I owe her a lot. But then someone contacted him to say that we should send someone to check on you." He smiled. "I shouldn't have been angry with you. It wasn't your fault."

"It's OK. I wasn't exactly friendly to you. I bet my cousins were involved in phoning your father," she said.

They were quiet for a while, listening to the wind and rain hit the window.

"It's difficult when you try to keep everyone happy," Lizzy said at last. "Sometimes I feel like I've spent my whole life trying to do what other people want me to do."

"Are you taking about your mother or Tom?" David asked, coming next to her at the table.

"Both, I think. Yes, after my dad died we had to sell our house. Mom was worried about money all the time. Even when I was a small child she encouraged me to think about what career I would go into. She wanted me to be secure, to have a steady job and money and a home. And then Tom came along, and he's exactly the nice, sensible kind of man Mom always wanted me to marry."

"But that's not what you want?"

"I don't know. That's the whole point. I've never had a chance to think about what I want."

"But you decided to accept Bea's challenge even when everyone told you not to. That was pretty brave."

"Yes but I'm still following someone else's plan. This time it's Aunt Bea deciding where I go and what I do."

David moved closer. "Do you think that you and Tom will get back together?" he asked.

Before Lizzy could answer, the door crashed open and they stepped away from each other. A large man in a rain jacket stood at the door. Behind him was a woman and two young men. They brought in the rain and wind with them.

"Good evening," he said with a smile. "I hope there is space for a few more people in here. What a terrible storm!"

The family was from Germany. The little hut was very crowded now. After eating, the family sat around the fire and sang songs. David and Lizzy joined in, smiling at each other across the table.

Chapter 10

The surprise visit

Lizzy was cycling downhill; after the storm it was a beautiful, clear blue day. There wasn't another human being in sight. Every part of her felt alive. Below her were green hills and lakes. The sound of her phone ringing almost made her fall off her bike. She found a safe place to stop. When she got it out, she realized that she had picked up David's phone by mistake. She answered it.

"Why on earth did you ask the police into my house?" her mother demanded. "All the neighbors are talking. They think I'm some sort of criminal."

"Where were you? I was worried." Lizzy wasn't sure whether to feel happy or angry to hear her voice.

"I decided to take a little holiday in Portugal. You're not the only one who is allowed to have an adventure, you know."

Portugal? Lizzy didn't even know her mother owned a passport.

"But why didn't you tell anyone? Richard and Justine were worried, too."

"Don't be silly. It was Richard who suggested that I take a little holiday to help me relax. He's such a thoughtful boy. And he was quite right; I feel like a new woman. Anyway, tell David I'm very angry with him."

Her cousins' attempts to worry her only made Lizzy more determined to finish the journey. They really were horrible, she thought, cycling angrily as the road started to go upward.

Well, she would show them.

At last the higher mountains turned into the baked earth of Provence. In her diary, Bea wrote: *The smell of lavender is all around me. I soon found work at a small lavender farm.*

But things had changed since her aunt's journey, Lizzy discovered. The small lavender farms her aunt described were now big businesses that no longer picked the plants by hand. Instead, Lizzy found work cleaning tables in a fast food restaurant in Antibes. She wiped up food and put cold hamburgers out with the rubbish. The owner was only employing her because she was traveling through, and he could pay her less than his other workers. She hated the way her clothes smelled of hamburgers.

David could see how much she disliked the work. That morning he met her at her campsite, saying, "It's only for a few days. Let me take you out to dinner tonight to cheer you up. I know this great little hamburger place." He grinned. Lizzy hit his arm lightly.

"OK, you can choose any restaurant you like."

Lizzy was cleaning the floor at work. She was looking forward to finishing and going out with David. The restaurant was empty, and the owner was about to lock the doors.

As she changed out of her uniform, she heard an English voice. Thinking it was David, she brushed her hair and went out to meet him.

"Hello, Lizzy." Tom was standing by the door. For a moment she was too surprised to speak.

"Are you going or staying?" the owner asked; he had the keys in his hand ready to lock the door.

In the street, they turned and looked at each other. Tom put his hands on her shoulders.

"Lizzy, I made a terrible mistake. I should never have let you go." He tried to take her in his arms.

"Tom, stop it. I don't understand. How did you know I was here?" She didn't wait for him to answer. "It was Richard, wasn't it?"

Tom looked confused. "Well, Richard gave me David's number, and I called him this morning. It was David who told me where to find you. None of this matters though, Lizzy. Your cousins told me how unhappy you were. I've come to rescue you."

"What did you say to David, Tom?" Lizzy asked.

"I told him that I was coming to find you and that we planned to get married."

Lizzy groaned. She looked at her watch. David should be here by now, but she knew that he wouldn't come.

"Come on, Tom. Let's go for a coffee. We need to talk," she said.

Chapter 11

The end of Daisy?

It took a long time to convince Tom that she didn't need to be rescued. It took even longer to explain that there was not going to be a wedding.

"When I left England, you said that I wasn't the same girl you asked to marry you. And you were right, Tom. Something has changed. I don't want to go back to a life where every day is exactly the same as the day before."

"Well, we could take more holidays," Tom suggested. "There's a football tour to Brazil next year. I have tickets; we could go together."

"Tom, did you know that I hate football?" Lizzy said quietly. She could see by the expression on Tom's face that this shocked him more than anything else she had said.

He insisted on walking her back to her tent in the campsite outside the town. The evening smelled of salt from the sea.

"I could change, you know," Tom said, turning to look into her eyes when they arrived at her tent.

"I don't want you to change. You're perfectly lovely as you are. We just don't fit together, and I think we've known that for quite a while."

He moved closer and took her hands. "My plane leaves tomorrow morning. Let me know if you change your mind," he whispered.

Before she could reply, Lizzy saw David on the path watching them. Without saying a word, he looked from Lizzy to Tom and then walked away.

73

Lizzy pulled her hands away from Tom and hurried toward the path, but David had already gone.

Tom followed her. "Is there something going on between you two?" he demanded.

She shook her head. "No, David's just a friend."

"Don't lie to me. I can see it in your face the same way I could see it in his. It really is good-bye this time." Tom walked angrily away.

Lizzy looked out into the summer night. In the distance she could hear the sea. She had never felt so confused. What exactly had Tom seen in David's face? Her heart was beating quickly as she took out her cell phone and tried David's number.

The phone rang and rang, but there was no reply.

As she cycled over the border from France into Italy, Lizzy didn't feel the happiness or pride that she had expected. For the last few days, David had hardly spoken to her. He was polite but cold. At the end of each day, he came and checked on her and then rode away on his motorbike. When she tried to talk about what had happened with Tom, he changed the subject. She cycled on angrily. Well, what did she expect, she wondered, a romantic celebration together when they reached Italy? Instead she had never felt more lonely. That evening, she set up her tent and felt the cool air blowing in from the sea. Why was she doing this stupid journey at all? She was angry with David, but most of all she was angry with herself. Looking up at the stars, she realized that she spent most of her life letting people tell her what to do: her mother, her boss, and Tom. Once again she was following orders like a good little girl, but this time she was following the orders of a dead woman. She looked down at Bea's diary and resisted a sudden urge to throw it into the sea.

Enough was enough.

On any other day, Lizzy would have admired the lovely town of Massa Di Marina. On one side there were mountains, shining in the morning sun, and on the other was the sea. But she was in no mood to go sightseeing. She called David's number. As expected, it went straight to messages.

"Hi, David, it's me. Can you meet me in Via del Cipressi in Massa? I want you to pick up Daisy. I don't want to do this anymore."

Next, Lizzy cycled into the center of town and found a travel agent. She glanced at a picture of London on a travel poster and quickly walked away. No, London was the last place that she wanted to be. She saw another poster with a picture of mountains in South America. That looked more interesting.

Outside there was the sound of an engine. She looked up to see a blue car speeding around the corner. There was a high scream of brakes followed by the sound of breaking glass. As she ran outside she saw that the car was exactly where she had parked Daisy. A young man opened the car door and got out, looking shocked. People surrounded him, talking and pointing.

She heard her name being called in panic and saw David running across the street and pushing his way through the crowd. He looked under the car, still calling her name. She hurried over and touched his shoulder. As he turned, relief lit his face, and he took her in his arms.

"I saw the bike on the ground. I thought the car had hit you." He held her close.

Her words came out in a rush. "I'm not marrying Tom. I should have told you that days ago, but you were so angry and I was angry, too."

"It's all right. I'm just so happy you're safe."

"No, let me finish, David. I was angry with Bea for making me feel all this confusion. Because I used to be so certain about everything, you see. Now I can't go back to my old life; it doesn't fit me anymore. But I'm not Bea, either. I don't want to be in her shadow anymore."

He smoothed her hair. "You made this your own adventure, Lizzy. It doesn't belong to Bea or anyone else now."

They bent and pulled the bicycle out from under the car. The front wheel was bent. A woman came over and spoke to David in Italian.

"She says she knows someone who can fix it. What do you think? It's your decision, Lizzy."

Lizzy touched the damaged bicycle and realized just how much she wanted to complete the journey.

"Yes, let's get Daisy fixed so I can finish this."

Carrying the bicycle together, they followed the woman down the street.

Chapter 12

The journey home

Daisy's blue and white paint didn't look so good after the accident, and the bell no longer worked, but after getting a new wheel she was ready to ride again.

"She's a tough old girl, just like Bea," David said.

It was the last part of the journey, down the Alpi Apuane mountains.

"Good luck. I'll meet you at Bea's farm," he said, kissing her good-bye. The downhill road was like a fairground ride. The wind was in Lizzy's hair, and every part of her felt alive. Little mountain lakes reflected back the summer sun. She stopped and washed off the dust from the road.

In the distance she could see the beautiful walled city of Lucca. And at the top of a hill surrounded by olive trees, she saw Bea's farm for the first time. The warm stone shone gold in the afternoon sun, and there were flowers outside the door. As she rode through the gates, chickens ran out of the way of her bicycle.

David ran over and kissed her. "Welcome home. Come and rest," he said leading her inside. Everything seemed like a dream. No more nights in a tent, no more tiredness and aching legs.

"No, I don't want to rest. Will you show me around?" she asked.

To her surprise, he shook his head. "No, it's your place now. Take your time and explore. I'll be in my cottage. Come over later and I'll show you some of the photographs I took on your trip."

The house was wonderfully cool after the heat of the afternoon sun. The furniture was simple. Lizzy looked around for signs that she was in Bea's house, but it didn't feel like that. It felt like home.

There was the smell of something good cooking, and she walked toward the kitchen. A woman was preparing food. For a moment she thought it was Bea. Then the woman turned.

"Mom?" Lizzy said in surprise.

"Congratulations, darling. You did it!" Her mother wiped her hands and hurried over to kiss her.

They sat in the garden and ate under the lemon trees. Her mother explained that David had asked her to come. "He thought there were some things we should talk about. He's a very good man, Lizzy." She asked Lizzy questions about the journey and seemed genuinely interested. Then she surprised her daughter by announcing that she was going on a trip of her own. "In three days time I'm leaving to visit my cousins in New Zealand," she said proudly.

After clearing away the plates, her mother asked Lizzy to follow her. They climbed the hill behind the house and sat on a rock surrounded by olive trees. There was a view across the hill to the lights of Lucca.

"David said that this was where Bea came when she wanted to think," her mother said. "I wanted to speak to you here because I hope that, somewhere, Bea can hear me too. It's about the letters."

"You don't have to do this, Mom." Lizzy saw the sadness in her mother's face and her heart ached.

"Yes, I do, Lizzy. It's important." Viola reached inside her pocket and took out some letters held together with string. "What I did was wrong. I know that now. I wanted you to be sensible, study hard, and get a good job so that you didn't have to worry about money the way I did. You had my love, but you didn't have much fun, I can see that now.

Bea tried to stop you being so serious all the time. You always had such a good time with her." Her mother sighed and shook her head. "And I suppose I was jealous. I thought you loved her more than me, you see. After our argument, Bea came to Italy. When she wrote, I hid the letters. I know how much it hurt her and how much it hurt you and I had no right to do it. I was just so afraid of losing you." Her mother was looking down. Lizzy reached across and took her hand.

"You can't ever lose me, Mom, and I know that Bea would understand, too."

"Bea would be so proud of you, and I'm proud of you, too, Lizzy." Her mother reached into her bag and took out a bottle of white wine. "This was made on Bea's farm," she said, pouring the wine into two glasses. They both stood up.

"To you, Aunt Bea." Lizzy raised her glass.

"And to adventure, wherever it may take us," her mother joined in. "Oh, Bea, I do hope you're having adventures wherever you are."

A cool wind whispered through the olive trees, turning the leaves to silver. For a second, Lizzy felt that her aunt was very near.

"Can I borrow Bea's bicycle?" her mother asked, packing away their glasses.

"Borrow Daisy? Sure. I've never seen you on a bike before, Mom."

"I'm not sure I can ride one. But it's not too late to learn, is it?"

"Of course it's not too late. It's never too late. What did Bea always say?"

"*Try something new every day,*" her mother laughed. "Oh, it did annoy me when she said that!" She looked at her daughter. "So are you going to stay here?"

Lizzy looked up at the stars in the sky above them. "I believe I'm going to take some time to decide what I want to do," she said at last.

"If I were you, I'd go back to London for your job and come here on weekends and holidays," her mother suggested. Lizzy reached out and gently put her finger against her mother's lips.

"But I'm not you, Mom. And I'm not Aunt Bea, either. I have to decide in my own time what I'm going to do, and the decision will be all mine. But one thing I am going to do is tell Mr. Carlton that I'm leaving my old job."

For a moment it looked as though Lizzy's mother had something to say about that, but instead she smiled.

"Whatever you decide is just fine with me, Lizzy. We all need to make our own way in life."

The night air smelled sweet. Lizzy held out her hand to her mother, and they walked together down the hill, back toward the house.

Her mother went to bed. Lizzy went into the living room, where she found a letter waiting for her. She immediately recognized Bea's handwriting. Taking it outside, she read:

> I always knew you could do it, Lizzy. I hope your journey has shown you how strong you are. And I also hope it has given you space to think. So often in life we do the same things day after day. The days become weeks and then months and then years. Sometimes we need a little time to consider if the life we are living is the life that we really want. Not everything in life can be planned; we need to learn to listen to our hearts. Now you have the rest of your life ahead of you, my brave girl, and I wish you many more adventures.
>
> Your ever-loving,
>
> Aunt Bea x

She put the letter down on the table and opened the door. Somewhere an owl was calling in the warm summer night. Down in the valley, a light shone in a window in David's cottage. Kicking off her shoes, she walked toward it across the warm red earth.

Review Chapters 1–4

A. Match the characters in the story to their descriptions.

1. _____ Viola   **a.** This person wants to marry Lizzy.

2. _____ Bea   **b.** Lizzy's male cousin

3. _____ Jane   **c.** Lizzy's mother

4. _____ Tom   **d.** Lizzy's friend and colleague

5. _____ David   **e.** Lizzy's female cousin

6. _____ Justine   **f.** Lizzy's aunt, who has just passed away

7. _____ Richard   **g.** This person accompanies Lizzy on her journey.

B. Number these events in the order that they happened.

1. Lizzy spends her first night in the forest.   _____

2. Lizzy and Tom break up.   _____

3. David and Lizzy travel to France.   _____

4. Her cousins offer Lizzy money not to do the challenge.   _____

5. Lizzy discovers Aunt Bea has died.   _____

6. Tom and Lizzy meet at their usual restaurant.   _____

C. Read each statement and circle whether it is true (T) or false (F).

1. Lizzy works in Paris.   T / F

2. Tom's favorite sport is football.   T / F

3. Lizzy's mom does not like Tom.   T / F

4. Lizzy has not seen Bea since she was a child.   T / F

5. David tells Lizzy that Bea died very suddenly.   T / F

6. Jane tells Lizzy not to accept Bea's challenge.   T / F

7. Tom and Lizzy end their relationship by e-mail.   T / F

8. David joins Lizzy for her first meal in the forest.   T / F

D. Circle the correct word to complete the summary.

Lizzy Elliot is tired of people thinking she is a(n) **1.** (independent / sensible)

girl. Her boyfriend Tom wants to start planning their **2.** (holiday / wedding),

but she is not very excited and wonders if Tom is the right man for her.

One day, her mom **3.** (calls / visits) to inform her that her aunt has passed

away. She meets David, a **4.** (lawyer / photographer) who was friends

with her aunt, and learns that Aunt Bea has left her some money and her

farm in **5.** (France / Italy). However, Lizzy must first complete a challenge

or everything will go to her **6.** (mother / cousins). In the end, Lizzy

accepts the challenge and travels to Fontainebleau by **7.** (train / car),

where she begins her journey. According to Bea's rules, she can't carry

any **8.** (bags / money) and must sleep in a **9.** (tent / hotel). David has to

follow her on his **10.** (bicycle / motorcycle) to make sure she doesn't cheat.

Review Chapters 5–8

A. Complete the crossword puzzle using the clues below.

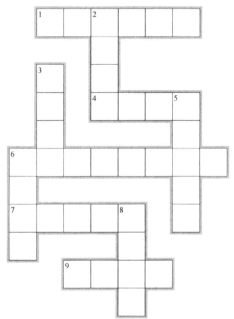

Across:

1. Lizzy steals some _____ from an orchard.

4. The workers must fill sacks with _____ to protect the wall.

6. Lizzy and David dance together at the town _____.

7. The workers are worried about the bad _____ coming.

9. Lizzy's cousins run off and leave her to pay the _____.

Down:

2. Lizzy wakes up and finds three little _____ outside her tent.

3. Marie-Helene thinks Lizzy is David's _____.

5. David gives Lizzy Aunt Bea's _____ to help her on her journey.

6. In the forest, Lizzy tries to catch _____ for dinner.

8. Marie-Helene makes Lizzy _____ the goats.

B. Choose the best answer for each question.

1. Why did Aunt Bea give Lizzy the challenge?

a. She wanted to make Lizzy's mom angry.

b. She didn't want to give her the farm for nothing.

c. She wanted Lizzy to meet David.

d. She wanted Lizzy to be adventurous.

2. What was the reason Lizzy never received letters from Aunt Bea?

a. Aunt Bea was angry with her.

b. Aunt Bea didn't know where Lizzy was.

c. Lizzy's mom must have kept the letters.

d. The letters must have gotten lost.

3. Which of the following is NOT a reason that Lizzy's cousins invited her to lunch?

a. They wanted to treat her to a meal.

b. They wanted to get her into trouble.

c. Lizzy's mom told them to check on her.

d. They wanted to offer her more money.

4. What did Lizzy do at the village near Bourg-en-Bresse?

a. She milked the goats.

b. She picked vegetables.

c. She helped out in a restaurant.

d. She helped to build the wall.

5. What do the workers NOT do with food from the garden?

a. They eat the food.

b. They give the food to city children.

c. They give the food to poor families.

d. They sell the food at the markets.

Review Chapters 9–12

A. Complete each sentence using the correct word from the box.

guilty	secure	confused	thoughtful
jealous	tough	relieved	aching

1. David is _____ that Lizzy was not hurt in the car accident.

2. Lizzy feels very _____ about what to do with her life.

3. Lizzy's legs are _____ from cycling up and down the mountains.

4. Jane tells Lizzy that she is _____ of Lizzy's exciting journey.

5. Lizzy's mother thinks that Richard is a very _____ boy.

6. Lizzy feels _____ for not contacting her mother during her trip.

7. All Lizzy's mother wanted was for Lizzy to be safe and _____.

8. David says the bicycle is very _____, just like Bea.

B. Read each statement and circle whether it is true (T) or false (F).

1. David works for his father.   T / F

2. David is meeting a girl in Italy.   T / F

3. Lizzy's mom went to Portugal for a holiday.   T / F

4. Lizzy sees lots of small lavender farms in Provence.   T / F

5. Lizzy does not like her job at the fast food restaurant.   T / F

6. Tom tells Lizzy that he is coming to meet her.   T / F

7. David thinks that Lizzy is going to marry Tom.   T / F

8. Bea's bicycle is not damaged at all in the accident.   T / F

9. Lucca is a small and peaceful place.   T / F

10. Aunt Bea wasn't sure if Lizzy would finish the journey.   T / F

C. Choose the best answer for each question.

1. Tom is very shocked when Lizzy says that she _____.

 a. doesn't like football

 b. is in love with David

 c. wants to quit her job

 d. doesn't want to marry him

2. Why did Lizzy almost give up toward the end?

 a. She wanted to go back and marry Tom.

 b. She was angry with David for being cold.

 c. She was too tired to carry on.

 d. She was tired of people telling her what to do.

3. Lizzy's mom didn't give her Aunt Bea's letters because _____.

 a. she thought Lizzy didn't want the letters

 b. she thought Lizzy loved Bea more than her

 c. she wanted the letters for herself

 d. she wanted to hurt Bea

4. Aunt Bea always said people should _____ every day.

 a. cycle

 b. meet new people

 c. try something new

 d. buy something new

5. By the end of the story, Lizzy decides to _____.

 a. go back to London

 b. travel to South America

 c. stay in Lucca with David

 d. quit her job and think about her life

Answer Key

Chapters 1–4

A:

1. c; **2.** f; **3.** d; **4.** a; **5.** g; **6.** e; **7.** b

B:

6, 4, 5, 3, 2, 1

C:

1. F; **2.** T; **3.** F; **4.** T; **5.** F; **6.** F; **7.** T; **8.** F

D:

1. sensible; **2.** wedding; **3.** calls; **4.** photographer; **5.** Italy; **6.** cousins; **7.** train; **8.** money; **9.** tent; **10.** motorcycle

Chapters 5–8

A:

Across:

1. apples; **4.** sand; **6.** festival; **7.** storm; **9.** bill

Down:

2. pigs; **3.** wife; **5.** diary; **6.** fish; **8.** milk

B:

1. d; **2.** c; **3.** a; **4.** b; **5.** b

Chapters 9–12

A:

1. relieved; **2.** confused; **3.** aching; **4.** jealous; **5.** thoughtful; **6.** guilty; **7.** secure; **8.** tough

B:

1. F; **2.** F; **3.** T; **4.** F; **5.** T; **6.** F; **7.** T; **8.** F; **9.** T; **10.** F

C:

1. a; **2.** d; **3.** b; **4.** c; **5.** d

Background Reading:

Spotlight on . . . *Lucca*

Lucca is a small city in central Italy, located in the region of Tuscany. It is very old—historians date it back to 180 B.C.—and still has many buildings which document its fascinating history.

The city is famous for one stunning feature—the ancient walls that

surround it. Back in the 16th century, its inhabitants built these broad and thick walls for protection. Today, people can walk (or cycle) on the wide and peaceful road which runs along the top of the walls.

Lucca itself is very small, and there are no busy roads with traffic. In fact, people are not allowed to drive cars in Lucca unless they live there. The city has lots of small, winding roads that lead to cathedrals, piazzas (open squares in the city), towers, and local shops and restaurants. Not many tourists visit Lucca, so most advertisements, signs, and menus are in Italian, and there are hardly any big shops. Many people who visit like to stay on farms in the countryside surrounding the city.

The pace of life in Lucca is leisurely compared to many cities. This means the speed at which people do things there is much slower than a place like London or Paris. People here prefer to walk or cycle, and many will stop to say hello and chat with their friends. You may also find them sitting in one of the many cafés reading the newspaper, sipping a coffee, or simply relaxing. In fact, *Forbes* magazine, in its September 2009 issue, picked Lucca as the most idyllic (simple and carefree) city in all of Italy and the second in all of Europe!

Life in Lucca

Cars are rarely seen in Lucca, and the best way to explore the city is on a bicycle. Tourists are not the only ones cycling either—you can see many young and old people going about their daily routines on bicycles.

Think About It

1. Why do you think Aunt Bea enjoyed living in Lucca?
2. Why do you think small towns and cities are more relaxed than big ones?
3. Would you rather live in a peaceful city, like Lucca, or a busy one, like London?

Glossary

cheat	(*v.*)	do things that are against the rules or are not honest
goat	(*n.*)	a farm animal with hooves, small horns, and long hair
hut	(*n.*)	small building made of wood
lavender	(*n.*)	plant that is used in perfume
lawyer	(*n.*)	person who gives advice about the law
lightning	(*n.*)	sudden bright light in the sky during a storm
metro	(*n.*)	train that travels under the ground
mud	(*n.*)	dirt that is wet and soft
olive	(*n.*)	green or black fruit from a tree that can be eaten or made into oil for cooking
orchard	(*n.*)	place where fruit trees grow
owl	(*n.*)	bird that hunts for food at night
piglet	(*n.*)	baby pig
pride	(*n.*)	feeling of satisfaction when you do something well
thunder	(*n.*)	loud sound during a storm when there is rain and lightning
sand	(*n.*)	very finely ground yellow pieces of rock found on beaches and deserts
sack	(*n.*)	large bag made from strong material
tent	(*n.*)	place to sleep; made from lightweight material and can be carried from place to place